YES YOU CAN
PUBLISH YOUR BOOK!

The Publicious guide to
Self-Publishing

1st EDITION

ANDREW MCDERMOTT

www.publicious.com.au

Yes You Can Publish Your Book
The Publicious Guide to Self-Publishing

1st Edition

First published in Australia 2018 by Publicious Pty Ltd
PO Box 395 Coolangatta Qld 4225 Australia
www.publicious.com.au

Prepublicatiuon Data available from the National Library of Australia
ISBN: 978-0-6482243-5-8   (ebk)
ISBN: 978-0-6482243-4-1   (pbk)

Typesetting/layout and cover design by Publicious Book Publishing
www.publicious.com.au

For you, the author

OTHER TITLES BY THIS AUTHOR

The Tiger Chase – fiction (2002, 2010, 2018)

The Last Tiger – children's fiction (2011)

The Galactic Knights – fiction (2014)

Flirting with The Moon – fiction (2018)

Quest of The New Templers – Book 1 – Resurection
fiction (2018)

Contents

Section Four

Section Five

Introduction

Welcome to *The Publicious Guide to Self-Publishing*, an author's handbook on today's complex and sometimes confusing world of the publishing industry. I'm Andrew (Andy) McDermott, founder and director of Publicious Book Publishing, a company I developed to help authors to understand the publishing process and to assist them to prepare their books for a global reading audience.

If you are an author with a manuscript, finished or in-progress, or you have been thinking about writing a book, this guide will provide you with valuable, industry-specific information and teach you the necessary skills that will simplify your journey towards publication.

Whichever type of writer you are or whatever genre, fiction, children's books, cookbooks and biographies etc, or perhaps your career as a blogger or a business owner/ entrepreneur has manifested into a possible self-help book, I'm certain that you feel strongly enough about your work that you would like it to be published. To that end, I offer this little book as the starting point to begin researching your publishing options.

As a writer myself, I congratulate you on all your hard work thus far. Completing a book is an amazing achievement – a truly remarkable accomplishment that few people attain. If you are still working on your manuscript or have just begun to consider writing your book, I applaud your grit and willingness to undertake such a task and being pro-active by exploring publishing options now.

This guide has been designed to address the areas of publishing that will affect you and your book. We will discuss what you'll need to do and more importantly what you mustn't do. We'll start at the very beginning of the process with all the necessary steps involved in bringing your book to publication, including: editing, typesetting, cover design, the necessary registrations and legal requirements, printing, ebooks, distribution and marketing. We'll also discuss in depth the varied publishing options available for the author of today.

The information in the following pages will help you avoid the pitfalls that have tripped up many self-published authors. Information I wish would have been available to me when I published my first book. It is a no-nonsense guide, designed to steer you through the minefield of publishing and help you make your book the best it can be.

Before we get started though, let me tell you a bit about myself and how this guide came into being.

Originally from Nottingham England, I've been an ex-pat English-Australian since 1989, living on Australia's fabulous Gold Coast. My first novel, *The Tiger Chase*, was published in 2002 with an American publisher. The book launch in San Diego was followed by a book tour of the US, including Las Vegas.

On my return to Australia, I soon became disillusioned with the publishing industry. I was locked into an unproductive contract, earning a tiny percentage of royalties for all my hard work, and didn't own any of my book's rights. This highly restrictive situation prompted me to pursue self-publishing with my later books.

I served as President of The Gold Coast Writers' Association (of which I am now an honorary lifetime member) from 2005-2007, working closely with like-minded authors by assisting them with their manuscripts and publishing needs.

In 2010, to mark the year of the tiger, I launched a revised and self-published edition of *The Tiger Chase* as a paperback and an ebook, donating all royalties to the Save China's Tigers Foundation.

That same year, I created Publicious Pty Ltd (www.publicious.com.au), a company designed to help authors, like myself, to get their books published.

I continue to write and have self-published my first, and last, children's book, *The Last Tiger. Flirting with The*

Moon is my detective novel following on from *The Tiger Chase* and was launched in 2018 with the sequel in the bottom drawer to follow. I'm currently working on the second book in a series of speculative fiction novels featuring *The New Templers*. I have taught creative writing at the ACE Adult Community College QLD and am active in the writing community, regularly speaking at writers' festivals and groups.

My experiences as a published writer led me to various publishing conclusions that became the foundation for Publicious Book Publishing and prompted the writing of this guide. I hope it will be a valuable asset to you in your pursuit of publication.

Good luck!
Andy McDermott

Your Manuscript

We'll start at the beginning: your manuscript. As this isn't a manual on writing, the assumption will be that you already know how to write and that you are here to explore your publishing options.

If your manuscript is in-progress or you are just considering the idea of writing a book, and feel uncertain about your writing abilities and skills, I would suggest seeking help through your local adult educational facilities. You can also research the many online writing courses that are available.

This section will help accomplished and prospective authors learn about the steps involved in preparing a manuscript for publication. It's very important to produce a body of writing that is the best it can possibly be before it begins it's publishing journey. And the best it can be is achieved through great writing and comprehensive, intelligent editing.

Let's see how this pre-publication phase works.

Editing – A Writer's Perspective

Writing the first draft of your manuscript is by far the most important phase of the writing process. This is when your creative juices are at their peak: the time when you give birth to your baby.

Depending on the type of book you are writing, you might go through a long hard labour or you might drop the little bugger before you reach the birthing suite. Either way, it is a unique and special time.

Like it or not, from the moment you finish your first draft, you have entered the editing phase. I remember what my first editor said to me when *The Tiger Chase* manuscript had been accepted for publication: "Congratulations, you've written a book, and you've got a publisher to take it on. You should be feeling pretty proud of yourself. Well, that's all very well, BUT NOW IS WHEN THE WORK REALLY BEGINS!" Although somewhat confused at the time by my editor's comments, in the years since I've come to understand exactly what he meant.

Most of my fellow fiction writers will know what I mean when I say how much I love writing that first draft. It is a glorious creative time when the story seems to flow from me, getting translated into keystrokes just as quickly as my fingers can move. This is the stage where grammar and punctuation and all those things that might distract my mind from the story's transmission are the furthest things from my thoughts. I've learned over the years how important it is at this stage to not get in my story's way. Just let it flow. Editing for me begins in the second draft. However, I realise we are all different and this may not work for everyone.

This is the birth of the first draft - the raw story - the bare beginning.

Unfortunately, too many novice writers believe that completing their first draft means their book is finished. This belief is far from reality.

I admit that with my first book I was certain that my first draft was *IT* - the best darn book ever written. Who dared to tell me any different?

Enter, my editor. Thank God! Along with learning that the work I had submitted, and was so proud of, was far from finished, I came to learn the invaluable lesson that editing should never, ever be overlooked. Remember, every successful writer uses the services of professional editors!

To clarify the importance of editing in making your book the best it can be, let's look at the three phases of editing:

- the self-edit

- the professional edit

- the proofread

The Self-Edit

Your first draft is complete. You have now reached the beginning, not the end, of the process of bringing your book into reality. Personally, when I reach the first draft stage I like to put the manuscript away for a bit – at least for a couple of weeks, longer if I can, months rather than weeks are better. It's a bit like a forced retirement, going cold turkey, taking a sabbatical, setting your 'baby' aside. Then, I find something else to work on, anything that will take my mind off the book.

This action can be difficult, but it is important to distance yourself from your book in order to begin the self-edit stage, with a more objective point of view. Resist the temptation to find validation by having anyone else read your first draft (first rule of edit club: nobody sees your first draft! Second rule of edit club: nobody sees your first draft!).

When you are ready to face your second draft, begin by reading through your manuscript, front to back. Be prepared to make notes: fill in any blanks that require research, remove clichés, and identify any areas that need rewriting, check grammar, punctuation, and correct word use. Do not rely on spell check to do this for you (example: waste/waist). Next, go back and perform any rewrites.

Congratulations! You are now the proud owner of a second draft. This is an accomplishment, however, a self-edit isn't confined to re-working and rewriting a single draft; it may need several. This process of re-reading and rewriting should continue until you have reached a draft stage you are happy with. You are now at the interim point in your self-edit where it's time to finally let someone else have a look (personally, nobody sees my work until at least the third draft).

When you make this move, seek the opinion of someone who will give your work an honest appraisal, not someone who will say your manuscript is wonderful just because they love you or don't want to hurt your feelings. This honest feedback is vital for you to learn the strengths and weaknesses of your book from a reader's perspective. If you are uncertain about finding such objective reviewers, check book clubs, writer's groups or associations, and colleges for people willing to be 'beta-readers' for your book. Many of these resources gladly support aspiring authors.

Carefully review all feedback and don't be upset if your readers don't like certain aspects of your story. Remember, you asked for their opinions so you could learn how others perceive your writing. It is now your job to decide which criticisms will help you improve your book. You make the call on how much you take on board – after all, it's your book – but you need to keep in mind that any writer that dismisses all critiquing out of hand, has not got their book's best interests at heart.

Now that your second draft has been reviewed, make your changes based on those reviews to create your third draft. Then, take another break from the story. When you feel 'clear' again, start the review process over: beta readers and their feedback, followed by rewriting/editing. Pursue your self-edit until you feel ready to take your manuscript to the next level of editing: the professional edit.

The Professional Edit

You may question the need for a professional edit, after all, you've read through your manuscript a gazillion times. You've had others read it again and again. You've made changes, corrected errors and typos, re-written and re-written - surely you've found and fixed everything?

The answer to that is: probably not. The fact that you know your story so well may mean that when you read through it, your brain transmits what it thinks is on the page and not necessarily what is actually written on the page.

You may have deleted or amended huge chunks of the story, changing scenarios in the course of rewriting that could now leave your future readers without important information or transitions. They can become lost by these confusing missing elements, such as when you tell them that Uncle Benny is actually Aunty Fanny. Oops, that's right; you deleted the chapter where Uncle Benny had his sex change. This might seem ridiculous, but it can easily happen (not necessarily Uncle Benny's sex change, rather the omission of back story). The potential for this type of confusion is why I like to take breaks between each draft to get my mind off the book. That way, when I return to it for the next self-edit pass, I'm reading it with fresh eyes.

Traditionally published books, like those you can purchase from good bookstores, are all professionally edited. Unfortunately, some self-published authors fail to pursue a professional edit. Most often, budget and time are the excuses given for overlooking this important step in the publishing process. While the cost of a professional edit can be substantial, depending on the amount of work required, it is a vital investment for which any serious writer should allow.

I'm amazed at the number of authors who don't think twice about paying for graphic design services to create an eye-catching cover, yet will quickly dismiss editing as an unnecessary expense. The truth is, a well-designed book cover may hook potential readers, but if the reader is subsequently disappointed with the quality of writing, they probably won't read past the first few pages. They also won't recommend the book to their friends or their book clubs. Whether their rejection is to not click on 'buy' or to shove your book back onto the shelf, the effect is the same: your book (and subsequent books) are not purchased, not recommended, and only remembered long enough to give a negative alert to other readers.

With this in mind, consider this question: if you write and publish another book, will the readers of your first book be likely to come back for seconds?

The professional editing process

Working with a good professional editor not only ensures that your book becomes the best it can be, but it also helps you become a better writer. You will be surprised at how much you will learn about writing, and shocked at the things that you've overlooked, during a professional edit. This is one of the great side benefits of this type of edit – for every writer who goes through it.

It's important to understand that it is not the editor's job to make changes to your manuscript or rewrite your work. A good editor will work closely with you, making suggestions as to how you can tighten and polish your writing style, as well as ways to improve the structure, flow, and characterisation within your manuscript.

Let's explore the steps and requirements of the professional editing process.

Typically, the following elements of your manuscript will be reviewed during a professional edit:

- overall structure and story arc

- character development and continuity

- sentence structure

- grammar and punctuation

- story flow, believability, strengths and weaknesses

- need for additional conceptual or environmental research

- identification of clichés, superlatives, ambiguities, and redundancies

You will also need to follow some industry-standard requirements when you submit your manuscript to an editor:

- Microsoft Word document (or similar program)

- A4 (US letter) size

- double spaced, single-sided

- 3 cm (1.18 inch) margins all around

- Times New Roman regular 12 point typeface

- numbered pages

- book title and author's name on each page

Most editors today expect Microsoft Word documents and accept email submissions. This is a digital-age boon to authors, saving time and expensive postage, as your manuscript can be sent as an email attachment. Email's global communication capabilities means you could just as easily be working with an editor on the other side of the world as on the other side of town.

Some editors still require a hard copy (paper copy) of your manuscript. If this is the case, print your manuscript and post it to the editor, enclosing a stamped, self-addressed envelope for its prepaid return. Notes and suggestions will be written in the margins by the editor, between the lines, and on the reverse of each page. In some cases, you will also receive a written report and telephone support.

Choosing the right editor for your book

There are some important factors to consider when choosing an editor. You wouldn't employ an electrical engineer to change the light fitting in your bathroom, nor would you use a brain surgeon to fix your teeth. The same principle applies to editing. You wouldn't choose an editor who specialises in academic work to edit a book written for young children or vice versa. So, choose your editor by determining their speciality or genre and by reviewing their qualifications and references.

The next consideration is cost. Editors can charge using per page or per hour rates. Personally, I dislike per hour rates for two reasons. Firstly, unless the editor contracts for a specific amount of hours, you have no idea how much the edit will cost until it is finished. This could result in a pricey surprise at the end. Secondly, you have no way of knowing how much time is actually spent in editing your manuscript. I prefer per page or per word rates because the editor can supply you with an accurate quote before you commit. Some editors will ask to see a sample of your manuscript, usually to determine the draft stage, and will provide an approximation of cost. No matter whether an editor charges by the hour or the page, you need to approach the cost of your edit as a business decision, taking your budget and your contractual rights into consideration.

Once the editor receives your manuscript they will begin the edit process by reading through your text. If the edit is in the form of a digital Word document, the editor will make notes in the comment boxes, and use the Track Changes feature, which allows for suggestions and deletions, as well as editorial questions and comments to be clearly visible on the page. Your manuscript is then returned to you with editor comments displayed in the right-hand margin. Deletions will appear within the right-hand margin and insertions will usually appear in red within the text. A good editor will read your manuscript with a critically trained eye, quickly picking up your writing strengths as well as your areas of weakness.

If the manuscript is a hard copy, the pages will be returned to you with hand written comments and suggestions.

Now, it's up to you to work through the editor's corrections and suggestions as you see fit.

Be Strong . . .

If you happen to believe that your book is above criticism, then don't submit it to an editor and instead just sit tight on your pedestal, telling yourself how good your book is. However, if you truly want your work to be the best it can be, check the thickness of your skin, take a deep breath, and dive into a professional edit.

> *"Whenever you feel an impulse to perpetrate a piece of exceptionally fine writing, obey it – whole-heartedly – and delete it before sending your manuscripts to press. Murder your darlings."*

This is a quote from renowned critic, scholar, and educational reformer, Sir Arthur Quiller-Couch in his 1916 book, *On the Art of Writing*. The phrase 'Murder your darlings' expressed the need for writers to be strong and delete passages that may have personal significance, but little or no relevance to the story.

Sometimes all it takes is a fresh pair of unbiased and experienced eyes to point out those things that aren't quite right or that you missed in all your self-editing efforts. You will thank your editor later.

Having said all this, however, the book is still your baby – you don't have to agree with all the suggestions your editor makes. The areas that are closest to you, the writer, are those that others, including the editor, may not understand. If you feel this is the case, after reviewing your edited manuscript, it is a good idea to step back and give the editor's suggestions some thought. If you decide there are certain parts you definitely want to keep, then consider rewriting them in a way that uses the editor's suggestions to make them clearer to the reader. Compromise is good.

Proofreading

After your edit you probably made extensive changes to your manuscript – from rewriting large and small sections to adding researched information to switching sentences, paragraphs, or even character attributes. Any changes you made will need to be reviewed by your editor, because try as you might, you won't see all the typos or the stray fragments of the sentences you deleted. Your editor's final proofread will ensure your work is error-free and polished.

Once your manuscript returns from being proof read, your professional edit is complete and you may rest assured that your story is as good as it can be. (Third rule of edit club: once your book is complete, don't read it again. Move on!)

All in all, self-editing, a professional edit, and a proofread are essential steps in making your book stand out from the millions of unedited books by unprofessional, self-published authors now flooding the market.

Your book deserves to be one in a million – doesn't it?

Which Type of Publishing?

I'm ready to publish my book/ebook. Where on earth do I start?

To find the answers you need, the best place to begin is by researching the different types of publishing and deciding which best suits your needs. In the following section, I have compiled some general information on commonly available publishing options.

1. Traditional Publishers

Most books at your local bookstore have been published through a traditional publishing house. This type of publisher usually acquires books as solicited manuscripts via literary agents. Their services are primarily performed in-house and include: editing, graphic design, type setting, printing, distribution, and marketing.

Advantages:

- Your title will receive the highest exposure and may be available for sale through high street bookstores.

- Authors do not pay traditional publishers to publish their book.

- Traditional publishers sometimes pay authors an advance prior to publication then pay a royalty percentage (usually 5 – 10% for the first-time author) from each sale.

Disadvantages:

- Traditional publishing can be difficult for first-time authors to break into, as it is more exclusive, most often supporting well-known authors and celebrities.

- Author advances are considered a loan that is paid back through sales of the book. No royalties are paid until the advance amount has been covered. It is important to know that an estimated 75% of first-time author books published using this option do not make sales over the advance figure. In some cases, when book sales do not cover the advance the author may have to return the balance to the publisher.

- Royalty percentages may be calculated after costs and not necessarily reflect a percentage of the recommended retail price (RRP). Books are supplied to bookstores by sale or return, and if sales are not forthcoming within 2-3 weeks, the title will be returned or discounted. This is why we see so many discounted books in the stores. And with each discounted stage, the author's royalty percentage can diminish.

- Authors have very little control of their books especially in areas such as design and sales.

- Authors can be locked into a contract.

- Authors are usually represented by an agent, who will take a further 10% of all earnings.

What are traditional publishers looking for?

There are some important things to understand before approaching a traditional publisher.

In most cases, publishers are looking to sign full time authors in the same way a plumbing company would employ a qualified plumber.

This means that once an author signs a contract with a publisher, the author will become the publisher's employee and be obligated to carry out all the necessary on-demand author tasks, such as book signings, interviews, speaking engagements, guest appearances, etc.

Authors are expected to build a brand that can be marketed, so publishers are interested in both the book and the author. What is the author's writing background? What accomplishments or awards have been earned? Is the writer active in the writing community? Could this writer produce at least one book each year? And, most importantly, is this author marketable?

A traditional publisher will take on a book only if they believe there is a market for it and that money can be made from it.

2. Partnership/Vanity Publishers

Partnership or Vanity publishers charge authors fees for limited editorial assistance, book production, and marketing.

Advantages:

- A good option for the author with a bottomless pocket, who isn't concerned with quality, sales, or having control over their book.

- Partnership/Vanity publishers make authors feel good or successful by telling them their books are great – regardless of the actual quality.

Disadvantages:

- This publishing option charges a high fee for services rendered, and takes around 80% of royalties for each book sold.

- Authors have very little control of their books and are usually locked into a 3-5 year contract.

- Acquisition processes are less selective and can result in flooding the market with low quality products.

- Few authors are successful using this publishing route, as they bear the cost and responsibility of marketing the book on top of the initial high set up fees.

- Marketing by the publisher is usually minimal, unless the author is prepared to pay additional fees.

What are some things to watch out for with Partnership/Vanity publishers?

If you decide to work with a Partnership/Vanity publisher, check the small print; make sure you understand exactly how much cost is involved and what you will receive for your money. Don't sign away all your rights and do try to negotiate a higher royalty for yourself.

If any publisher tells you your book will be a success or even goes as far as guaranteeing it will become a bestseller (I've seen this advertised on some websites) – walk away.

While serving as President of a large writers' association, and more recently as a publishing consultant, I have met many writers who have had the misfortune of being stung by this type of publisher. Often this happened because they hadn't understood what they were signing or, even worse, they had simply been ripped off. The cost to authors can amount to thousands of dollars.

3. Self-Publishing

Self-publishing is when the author of a book/ebook takes on the role of publisher and is responsible for the production, marketing, and distribution.

Although self-publishing has been around for many years, the exposure now available via the internet, online global distribution, and the convenience of Print On Demand (POD) has brought this form of publishing to the forefront. It has become the first choice of even previously, traditionally published authors.

Advantages:

- Authors have full control over their book, earn 100% royalties, retain all of their rights, and are not bound by a contract.

- Marketing, if undertaken properly via the Internet and social media, does not have to be expensive, and if conducted with a POD distribution system in place, titles can be available for sale worldwide.

- Professional assistance, including editing, graphic design, typesetting, printing, online distribution, and marketing can be obtained to create a book that can compete with anything in the bookstores. You needn't do all the work yourself.

- Authors can print as few or as many copies of their books as required at a wholesale price.

Disadvantages:

- Authors are responsible for all costs included in the production and marketing of their book.

- Achieving strong sales can be difficult unless authors are willing to put in the effort required, such as author personal appearances, book signings, and on-going marketing.

- If authors cut corners in an attempt to save time and money, their book will likely be of a poor quality.

What makes self-publishing an author-directed experience?

Self-publishing works very well, as long as the author is well-informed, understands their role as publisher, and has realistic expectations. Authors anticipating strong book sales just because the title is available worldwide on Amazon will be very disappointed. The more effort an author puts into publishing their book, the greater their return.

4. Ebook Publishing (self-publishing)

Ebook publishing is the newest type of publishing and the most cost affective, as there are no print costs involved. If distributed properly, titles can be available for instant download to ebook readers like Kindle, iPad or Nook from most online ebookstores.

Ideally, books should be converted to the Electronic Publication (EPUB) format.

Advantages:

- Assistance with ebook conversion and distribution is available and affordable.

- Authors can expect to earn 100% royalties after costs.

- Ebookstore mark-ups are generally lower (30 – 55%) than high street bookstores for print versions (50 – 70%).

- Ebooks can be sold cheaper, making them an attractive option for buyers.

- Ebooks are tremendous ancillary products that can support an author's brand, career, and future books, as well as being used as a low-cost marketing tool.

Disadvantages:

- Ebooks must be converted to the proper format and a cost is involved if the author is unable to convert the files.

- Ebooks may display differently than the original formatting on some ebook readers, especially older versions.

- Ebooks need to be priced low to attract buyers.

5. Online Publishing

Online publishing opportunities can include posting articles, short stories, novellas, or even novels (perhaps in chapter instalments) on an author's website. Author blogs also provide an online venue for presenting work. Websites representing writing associations and schools, book clubs, and other writing-related groups may also offer free space where authors may post their material.

Which type of publishing is for you?

As you consider your publishing options, there are a few things to bear in mind with each.

Traditional Publishing:

- Most traditional publishers do not accept unsolicited manuscripts, so you will need a literary agent.

- Most literary agents do not accept unsolicited manuscripts, due to the huge numbers of manuscript submissions.

- Some publishers and agents will only consider first-time authors through referrals from a well-known, traditionally published author.

- Traditional publishers usually only accept manuscripts produced by authors with proven writing credentials and concise samples of their work.

If you are adamant about choosing traditional publishing, expect to receive a few rejection slips (most authors have), then take note of what I said about being a full time writer and go for it. Don't give up until you have realized your dream. Good luck!

Partnership/Vanity publishing:

- Shop around for the best deal.

- Understand that you may be signing over all your rights and around 80% of your royalties for a period of up to 5 years.

- Do not sign a contract unless you are absolutely certain of the terms and agreements.

- Make sure you are fully aware of what the publisher is supposed to be doing for you.

Self-Publishing:

- Suitable for all kinds of writers.

- Authors retain rights, full control over their book, are not retained under contract, and earn 100% royalties.

- Publication support services are available that allow you to achieve a high quality product that can compete with traditionally published works.

Have you written your memoir and only want to print a few copies of a quality hardback book for family and friends? Are you an entrepreneur or an expert in your field who requires a printed book to sell at conferences or seminars? Do you have an ebook to either sell or give away via your website? Perhaps you are an artist or photographer and would like to produce a coffee table book. Then again, maybe you are a children's writer, with a series of books ready to delight young readers – or a novelist building your brand and wanting to sell your fiction to the world. Whatever your needs, there has never been a better time to take advantage of the benefits and flexibility of self-publishing.

The changing face of publishing

The publishing industry is going through a time of enormous change. With the inexpensive options of Print On Demand (POD) and online bookstores, authors can self-publish their books and ebooks and distribute them worldwide without the need for and hassle of traditional publishers.

It's impossible not to notice how many high street bookstores are closing down as a result of more and more buyers purchasing books online and downloading ebooks to an array of digital devices. This ever-expanding situation is bad news for the publishing houses and bookstores, but music to the ears of self-published authors who would otherwise never have a chance of seeing their titles stocked in the bookstores. It also opens lucrative opportunities for experienced authors who, in the past, have been rejected and, in some cases, belittled by the traditional publishing houses.

Self-publishing is no longer a last resort alternative used by authors who were unable, for one reason or another, to publish traditionally. It is now a booming industry which showed an amazing 287% growth between 2006 and 2011, and a further 60% growth in 2012. These figures continue to grow yearly. This is why self-publishing is becoming the first choice of most authors and entrepreneurs.

I want to self-publish – what's next?

If, you've decided that self-publishing is the way for you to go, where do you start? You've heard terms like ISBN, CIP, Legal deposit, POD, ebook formatting, online distribution, social media marketing, and (take a deep breath) – you're finding it all a bit overwhelming.

Well, read on and I will endeavour to answer all your questions.

From Manuscript to Book

Congratulations, you've chosen to self-publish... Now what?

This section will take you through the many processes of self-publishing and introduce you to the terms, phrases, and requirements that are involved. From now on, you are no longer just an author – you are now an author/publisher!

Getting Started

To begin with you need to decide how involved you want to be in the design and creation of your book/ebook. Some authors are comfortable with taking complete control over their project and are willing to learn the process from start to finish. Others may find the idea totally overwhelming, preferring to hire a professional to take care of the design work.

As an experienced self-published author, I would recommend working with professional designers to ensure that your book's appearance is of a high enough quality to be competitive with the millions of other books vying for readers' attention. Using the skills of such professionals doesn't mean you can't remain in control. Whoever provides this kind of support on your book will be working for you, because in self-publishing, you are the boss.

If you do decide you would prefer to have trusty and experienced professionals take care of the design and publication of your book/ebook, skip on to Section 5 to discover how Publicious can assist you.

Typesetting

If you have decided to do your own design, I offer the following thoughts and recommendations:

The first task you will face following editing is typesetting, which is the process of converting your manuscript to a book layout.

Many authors use Microsoft Word when writing their manuscripts and attempt to typeset their book using the same program. Most find this to be very frustrating and difficult. MS Word is great software for writing, but it isn't designed for typesetting. If you are determined to perform your own typesetting, my advice is to acquire Adobe InDesign, the recognised industry standard in publishing software. You will need to invest a small amount of cash (shop around and pick up CS6 or later for around $200) and undergo quite a learning curve, but if you are willing to persevere, your hard work will pay off.

Once you are ready to start with InDesign there will be a number of steps in the typesetting process. The basics will go something like this:

- Create a book file and call it 'Your book title-text'.

- Open a new page and set the size that you want your finished book to be, for example A5, then name it 'template'.

- Calculate approximately how many pages there will be in a typical chapter and add the necessary blank pages (you can add or delete pages later if you need to when you add text).

- Make sure you have the text flow function turned on and the pagination set to automatic.

- Set your styles in the template, e.g. 'Header 1' for chapter headers, 'Header 2' for sub-headers, 'Paragraph 1' for basic paragraphs, etc.

- Don't use Sans Serif fonts for printing. Only use Serif fonts as they are easier on the eye with an exception of Times New Roman. Use this font for writing but not publishing. The most widely used font for publishing nowadays is Adobe Garamond Pro. Try not to use fancy fonts as this can make your book look amateurish and hard to read.

- Save the template as 'Chapter 1'.

- Import or copy and paste your text from the Word.doc.

- Add 'Chapter 1' to the book file, then repeat the process for the rest of the chapters.

Any images or photographs will need to be 300 dpi (dots per inch) or higher resolution CMYK (4 colour – Cyan, Magenta, Yellow, and Key-black) for printing or 100 dpi RGB (Red, Green, Blue) for ebooks. Images will need to be resized (I recommend using Photoshop) and placed in image boxes. Text can be easily wrapped around images where necessary and captions can be added using text boxes.

If you are using photographs in your book, it is important to ensure that you have the necessary permissions to publish them. Don't download or copy photographs from the internet or from other publications with the assumption that you can use them. Those images will have copyrights in place and restrictions on their use. So be certain that the source of the photograph has no intellectual properties attached, e.g. celebrities etc. However, if you have taken the photographs, you own the copyrights.

Book cover design

People often talk about the importance of a book's cover design, alluding that a great eye-catching cover can attract buyers and influence their decision to purchase the book. It is true that a well-designed cover is critical to your book having a professionally published appearance, but remember, self-published books are rarely displayed in the high street bookstores. Buyers on the internet browse online bookstores differently than they would a high street store. In most cases, they already have an author or title in mind, or they are searching by keywords or phrases (see book marketing). The book cover design remains a vital selling point online, but its impact can be reduced. We all love a great book cover and we all want our book to look the best it can, but we need to keep the reality of what makes our book a great book firmly in the forefront: the content. It is vital to remember that this is what you spent months, and for some of you, years working on – writing and rewriting. Unfortunately, some self-published authors forget this essential point and chose to skimp on vital components such as editing, in favour of an expensive book cover design.

Having said all that, here are my tips for creating a great design – and remember, you shouldn't have to mortgage the house to get a great cover:

- Unless you are an experienced artist or graphic designer, don't try to create your own illustrations for your cover, hire a professional.

- If you have some experience with Photoshop or InDesign or similar software, you can create an eye-catching design by layering photographs that you have taken or have purchased from an online royalty-free stock photography site (see list of royalty free photograph providers on the resources page). You can also source, images, logos and illustrations on these sites.

- Make sure you have the necessary permissions to use any photographs that you haven't taken yourself and be familiar with the copyright terms and conditions of use.

- For printing, you need to create a separate file for the cover incorporating the front, back, and spine. To achieve the correct spine thickness, decide which type of paper you are using for the interior pages, then calculate the thickness of the desired paper with the number of pages (you may need to contact your printer to find out the paper thickness).

- Make sure all images are high-resolution. Fix your ISBN barcode to the back cover, then create a PDF/X file. This will insure that all images and fonts are automatically embedded. If you are unable to produce a PDF/X file, a standard PDF will suffice; you'll just have to make sure that images and fonts are embedded.

- A 3mm bleed all round is required for the printer, along with crop marks. This is to insure that if the book trimming is slightly out of line, it will not be noticeable. If there were no bleed, a white edge would appear.

Ebook Formatting

The three most common formats for ebooks are EPUB, MOBI and PDF.

- EPUB (Electronic Publication) is the most widely used ebook format and is readable on most ebook readers, including the iPad, Android tablets, and smartphone devices. The advantage of EPUB is that it allows text to fit any sized screen. This means that if the font is set at 12pt, it will remain that size whether displayed on a tablet or computer screen or a smartphone. This eliminates the need to zoom-in to read text. EPUB also has interactive capabilities that allow the reader to change the size or type of the font, etc.

- MOBI is the format used by Amazon for their Kindle devices. Although this format appears similar to an EPUB, it is limited in that it is available only for Kindle and MobiPocket readers.

- PDF is the oldest ebook format and still used by many publishers for free downloads from their websites. A PDF works well for reading on a computer, but because it is a fixed format, it will not have the interactive capabilities that are available for EPUB and MOBI.

If you know how to create a PDF, you can easily make an ebook in this format using Microsoft Word or Adobe

InDesign. You can also create EPUB files using InDesign, but at this time, I wouldn't recommend it. For me, the end result is just not good enough.

To create professional EPUB and MOBI files, I strongly recommend hiring an ebook conversion company. This should work out to be inexpensive and quick, plus it will give you the piece of mind that your ebook will display correctly on as many devices as possible.

ISBNs

An International Serial Book Number (ISBN) is required for all books and ebooks that are to be made available to the public for sale. A separate ISBN is also required for each individual format of the same book, such as softcover, hardcover, ebook and audio. ISBNs are issued by the ISBN agency, Thorpe and Bowker.

When first applying for an ISBN, you will need to open an account with Thorpe and Bowker, register yourself as a publisher, and pay an initial publisher set-up fee. If you are publishing a book and an ebook or if there will be future books, my advice would be to purchase your ISBNs in blocks (minimum block of 10). This is a much more affordable option. All the numbers will belong to you and there is no time limit for their allocation.

After purchasing your ISBN, you will need to allocate it to your book/ebook. To do this, log-in to your Thorpe and

Bowker account and complete the online form by entering your book's details (metadata). Upload a PDF copy of your book and a jpeg image of the front cover. In the metadata you will be required to include the information that you want to appear in the database, such as the recommended retail price (RRP), book size, page count, etc.

You can also purchase and download your ISBN barcode from your account ready for placing on your back cover.

Recommended Retail Price (RRP)

An RRP is the retail price that the publisher/author will need to set for their books and ebooks. Remember though, this is only a recommended price; bookstores can actually charge whatever they like. If you are working with a distributor make sure that your royalty is set. This protects you from being out of pocket if bookstores sell your book/ebook at a discount.

Prepublication Data Service (formerly CIP)

The Prepublication Data Service (formerly known as Catalogue-In-Publication or CIP) is a free service offered to publishers by the National Library of Australia to provide a catalogue record for newly-published books (for clients outside Australia, check out your National Library website for information). To take advantage of this service, you will need to fill out an application form on the National Library website (see resources page for relevant links). Registrations cannot take place without a current ISBN.

Applications are submitted online and are generated instantly. The details of which will be emailed to you to be included on your copyright page should you choose to do so.

Printing

When looking for a printer for your book, choose one that specialises in books. Do not use printers, high-street or otherwise, that normally handle print jobs such as stationary, flyers, or other non-bound products. This choice will prove to be costly and the end product may be disappointing. Printers that specialise in books will have a range of paper types to choose from and should be able to produce the kind of quality book that is expected by bookstores and libraries.

You can also decide how many books you want printed at a time. Higher quantities will normally offer larger discounts but don't purchase a large quantity of books just because you'll get a lower unit price. Only do this if you know you can sell the books. Depending on your circumstances I would recommend printing a small run to start with, say 50 - 200, and test the market first. You will pay a higher unit price but at least you won't be stuck with a couple of thousand dollars worth of books in the garage that you can't sell.

Another good aspect of purchasing only a small quantity is that if you need to make changes to the book at anytime you can do it easily. You can also use these books for obtaining reviews.

Short run printing utilizes digital printing, higher quantities (usually 1000 plus) is offset printing. The difference is the size of the machinery and the process. Although offset printing is arguably a higher quality, digital printing is evolving and makes such systems like Print On Demand (POD) possible.

Most printers will also allow you to purchase an advanced proof copy or a mock-up of your book. There is usually a fee involved but this is a good option if you want to check that everything is right with your design before going to print.

Legal Deposit

Legal Deposit is a requirement under the Copyright Act 1968 for publishers and self-publishing authors where one copy of any work published in Australia must be deposited with the National Library and one copy to your State Library (where applicable). Legal Deposit ensures that Australian publications are preserved for use now and in the future.

As an author/publisher this is your responsibility, so when you receive your printed books, be sure to send the required copies to The National and State Libraries (see resources page for relevant links).

If you have published your title as an ebook only, you can submit your metadata and files via the National Library website.

You need only submit one format of the title, either ebook or print.

Book database listings

Bookdata listings are a great way of giving your book the best exposure possible.

Bowkerlink

The Bowkerlink World Book database is the resource widely used by bookstores, schools, and libraries worldwide for purchasing books or accessing book information.

When you purchase an ISBN, your listing in the Thorpe and Bowker database is automatic in your country of publication. You can easily enhance your listing though, by adding these extra markets: US, UK, Canada, Europe, and New Zealand. Best of all, it's free! (see resources page for relevant links).

Nielsen Book Database

This book database is used by an increasing number of shops and organisations for ordering books. It can work in conjunction with the Bowkerlink Database and may be an advantageous option you would want to consider (see resources page for relevant links).

Online Global Distribution – how does it work?

Not so long ago, a self-published author would have to print a large quantity of books, then post them out, one at a time, whenever a sale was achieved. This was very costly; especially if sales were being made overseas. With the varied options for online global distribution, this expense and limited delivery is now a thing of the past.

Print On Demand (POD) – works in conjunction with online stores so authors no longer have to purchase a stock of their books or worry about the high cost of postage.

When a buyer purchases a book through one of the online stores, such as Amazon or Barnes and Noble, that one book is then printed at the POD facility closest to the buyer and posted to the buyer at the buyer's expense.

Taking advantage of this method of book distribution launches your book to the world market and ensures it is for sale 24/7. Have you ever purchased a book from

Amazon or one of the similar online stores? If so, that is exactly how this system will work for your overseas sales.

When you realise that everything, such as invoicing and postage, is taken care of for you, it's easy to see the advantages of this distribution model. However, it would be very difficult for self-published authors to set up such a system on their own. Imagine trying to create accounts with all the online stores (with all the tax implications involved), as well as organising POD printers around the world who will agree to one-at-a-time on-demand printing of your books.

Thankfully, Publicious can assist you in navigating the online global distribution of your book.

Ebook distribution – works the same as POD distribution, but without the obvious need for printing. Ebooks distributed through online stores such as Amazon (Kindle), Apple iTunes/iBooks, KOBO and Booktopia etc are available for instant download anywhere in the world.

POD and Ebook Distribution – Australian authors can work directly with large US companies, such as CreateSpace (Amazon) and Smashwords, but there are a few things to keep in mind:

- Royalties will only be issued by cheque and only after achieving a certain amount of sales.

- Authors will need to obtain a US tax number;

otherwise, the IRS will withhold tax at the highest percentage.

- There can be difficulties, delays, and unforeseen costs when banking cheques from overseas.

- Dealing with a large US company can be difficult or cumbersome.

After dealing with all these issues, authors are often left wondering: is it really worth it?

Fortunately, there are companies that can help you, but be careful and do your research before signing up with any publishing provider. Read the small print and make sure you understand any documents, agreements, or contracts you are signing.

For more information on POD and ebook Global Distribution, call Publicious on 1300 301 591 or send an email to: mail@ publicious.com.au or visit https://www.publicious.com.au/ distribution.html

Book Marketing

This is the big one, the one thing all self-published authors want to know is: 'How do I market my book?'

Before we discuss this topic in depth, I'd like you to read the following article with an open mind:

The Tale of Three Bobs

Bobby, Robert and Bob are self-employed plumbers who also sell their own (plumbing) products. Each man is around the same age, but each steers their plumbing career differently.

Bobby is a motivated man who loves being a plumber and he is open minded - especially when it comes to learning new ways to promote his plumbing service and his products. Bobby learned early in his plumbing career that being a good plumber wasn't enough, and that to be successful he would need to build a brand and take control of the sale of his products. Nobody was going to do it for him and there was no 'Magic System' that would market his products.

Bobby invested in an impressive website and hired a team of experts to assist him with his online presence to ensure that his site would be found.

Twice a month he writes a blog covering simple topics from how to fix a leaky tap, to finding the right plumber for the right job. He uses social media sites: Facebook, Twitter, Linkedin and Instagram to get his message out and to sell his products. He even shoots his own informational videos using his smart phone and regularly uploads them to his website for free and posts them on YouTube.

The work is time consuming but after a period of time his blog has gained a large following and Bobby is now a known, respected and sought after plumber. Soon he will be able to hire a company to run his social media and blog, leaving him more time to spend on new products and increasing his brand.

Robert is a good plumber but he has old-fashioned ideas. His full name is Robert L. Smith, which he displays proudly above the word Plumber on his home-made business cards. This is the extent of his brand. Although he is self-employed, he dreams of one day working for one of the big companies so that he won't have to work so hard anymore. He believes it will just be a matter of time before one of those companies will hear how good a plumber he is, and they'll make him an offer that will change his life forever.

Robert has a website that a friend built for him for free some years ago, but it hasn't been updated in all that time, it isn't user friendly and it can't be found on the search engines, so it receives no visitors. Because of this, Robert has come to the conclusion that websites are a waste of time and money.

Robert hates social media. 'Facebook, huh, why do people feel the need to want to tell everyone what they're doing?' he says. He isn't interested in how social media could work for his brand. He doesn't know that he can have a page on Facebook for his products or that writing a blog could help him sell more products. The truth is that the technology scares him a little so he shuns it.

Robert picks up work here and there, and if he's lucky he gets to sell a few products every now and then. Robert believes that he should be allowed to concentrate on plumbing and leave the marketing of his products to someone else. Because of his attitude, he's wasted time and money while constantly looking for that 'Magic System' and he's even been ripped-off by companies who promised to market his products.

Bob is a handyman plumber and he also sells a few products here and there. He's aware of social media networking and the importance of having a website, but he hasn't bothered to build a brand. Deep down he knows that he could be more successful and that his lack of motivation to succeed is holding him back, but he doesn't care.

Everybody tells him how great his products are and that they can't understand why he isn't more successful. The truth is, Bob enjoys what little work he gets and sees his plumbing as more of a hobby than a job.

***

If you haven't figured it out already, I want you to go back and read the article again but this time change the words plumber to writer, plumbing to writing, and products to books. Then ask yourself, honestly, which Bob are you?

Beware the book marketing trap!

As a self-published author and director of Publicious, I used to spend time looking for that magic bullet that would not only fire my own books to success, but also those of my clients. Through my own experiences I soon realised that it didn't exist and, just like any other author, I needed to get out there, build a brand and sell *myself* as well as my books.

In my early days I was tempted by so called Publishing Providers (you may have seen them on the net) who make ridiculous claims about how they can successfully market a book without even seeing it first.

All I can say about such companies is: beware! In my opinion, it's best to stay clear of them.

So — as you do your research on marketing companies/ publishing providers, avoid any that:

- Promise to make your book a best seller.

- Claim that your book will be available in all the high street bookstores.

- Make claims such as: 'We'll take care of the marketing leaving you to do what you enjoy best, writing.' This would imply that authors have no part in marketing their books. Wrong! Whether you are a traditionally published author or a self-published author, you will need to be out their marketing yourself and your book.

- Offer to write and send out press releases. A poorly written press release can actually do you and your book more harm than good. Any releases that might be written are usually sent to generic email lists, along with thousands of others, and end up unread in spam filters.

- Charge you a large sum of money to display your book at one of the international book fairs. Book fairs are primarily developed as marketing venues for the larger publishing houses, so they can display their wares and negotiate international rights. Your book will be sitting on the shelf of a cheesy little stand, inside a huge hall, with hundreds of bigger and better stands displaying thousands of books.

It's unlikely it will even be seen. If you have been considering this as an option – don't!

- Make ridiculous promises. You'll know them when you hear them.

If you have the budget, but not the time, to market your book you can hire a promotion company to handle it for you. Again, this is a business decision, so do your research before making this kind of choice. Make sure you understand what the company is providing in terms of services and that their experience includes marketing books. Many marketing firms can tailor a campaign to your budget, but may require you to commit to a minimum campaign time frame, such as 3 months.

Marketing options can also include radio and TV appearances. If you can organise these yourself, you'll save a lot of money. Otherwise these avenues do not come cheap, and though seemingly powerful, they may not be the best approach for your circumstances.

Regardless of the option you choose it will still mean that you'll be required for interviews, signings and appearances. So make sure you are ready.

What can I do on my own to market my book?

Take heart, there's never been a better time for self-published authors to promote their books worldwide and, in most instances, it can be absolutely free! You may even find that you really enjoy working with the many creative and exciting self-marketing options that are available.

Website

It's important to understand that your readers will be interested in your book, but will also want to know about you, the author. To feed this interest, you will need a platform on which to build your brand. The best place to start is by creating a website devoted to you and your book. This one marketing step is a must for all authors. Imagine it as your shop front – and it's open 24/7 to the world.

Creating a website doesn't mean you have to spend thousands of dollars. In fact, depending on your requirements and know how, you can set up a basic site for free. At this point, you need to decide how much work you want to do yourself, how much you are willing to outsource, and how serious you are about sales.

If you are aiming to attract prominent prospective readers, your website will need to be impressive enough to make them want to buy your book. Buyers are not interested in amateurs who have produced a mediocre website. In fact, this may give them the impression that your book will be of a similar quality and put them off.

Unless you have substantial web-building skills or the time to learn them, I would recommend having a professional web designer build your website. The price for an effective, reader-friendly site should range from $500 to $2500, depending on your needs. The lower price would usually include five pages: Home, About the Author, Book (synopsis, book cover image, etc), Bookstore (purchase options), and Contact. In the future, you can add pages for your new books, your blog, guest bloggers, or press releases and news about you or your books.

You can also create your own website using Wordpress or Joomla or WIX.com etc. These website-building programs are also used by pro-site builders to excellent effect. If you choose to go it alone, be prepared to undergo a fairly steep learning curve and to put in a substantial amount of time (see resources page).

You will need to open a PayPal account, if you haven't already. It's free and is by far the best, cheapest, and easiest way to make transactions over the net. (see resources) Once your account is set up you are ready to sell books from your website.

If your book is included in the POD/ebook distribution channels (see page 39) you can also include links to the stores, such as Amazon, and direct traffic to them via a buy-now button on your site. This is a great option if you don't want to be posting out books and it can work hand-in-hand with your distribution model.

You may have heard the term "SEO" (Search Engine Optimisation) used in relation to websites. SEO is an important and particular way of presenting website content so that primary search engines, namely Google and Bing, recognise and rank your site. Doing SEO effectively means ensuring that your website is displayed in the first page (preferably) when your name, your book's title, or relevant search terms are entered by an internet user. A lot of time and money can be spent chasing Google's ever-changing SEO algorithm requirements, but a good web designer can give you a solid SEO start. From there, you will need to make sure your pages are regularly updated with new content to refresh search engine recognition. A blog is a great way of doing this, as well as press releases, new book reviews, or even video trailers.

Alternatively you can subscribe to Goggle Adwords, which (for a fee) will automatically place your webpage on the first page of Google for a certain time period (see resources page). This can in some cases work out cheaper than hiring an SEO firm.

Blogs

You're a writer, so what better way to get the word out about your book than to write about it? Basically, a blog is a way of writing and publishing short articles online – and you control the content. Wordpress is a great platform for setting up a blog, either within your author/book website or as a standalone blog site. Write about what you know, share your articles with others, invite guest bloggers, and link your blog to other sites and blogs. Maintaining a blog takes some effort, but is a great (and free) way to market your work and get involved with the online writing community.

Articles

Writing articles and posting them online will help lift your profile and build your brand. Articles are usually associated with non-fiction books, but even a novel may have a central theme. If you write a detective story set in 19th century London or the modern day outback of Australia, no doubt you will do a fair bit of research to make sure your story is accurate. Why not use your research to write articles? These articles will be directly relevant to your story and can be posted on your website or in your blog. There are also websites that offer free space to display your articles. If you post to such sites, be certain that at the bottom of each article you include your author details, a copyright symbol, and a link to your website. These kinds of posts can drive traffic to your website and produce the quality links that support strong SEO.

Forums

Forums are another way for an author to get involved with the writing community. There are literally thousands of forums on the net covering just about every topic. Explore, find the groups that interest you, and join up. Then, get involved in discussions, but be respectful and professional at all times. Don't go in big-noting yourself and don't be baited by group members who express views that differ to your own. Some forum group members can be outspoken and can even turn vicious when challenged. In my experience, such people are usually wannabe writers with nothing better to do than sit on the net all day, searching for conflicts. They are easily spotted and best avoided – you want your forum experiences to enrich your contacts, your writing, and ultimately, your brand.

Book reviews

Book buyers read book reviews. That's a fact. So, it is important to get as many positive reviews as you can. One way to do this is to research reviewers for your genre and send a polite query letter to each one. This eletter should briefly tell the reviewer about you and your book. Keep it short and sweet or it won't get read.

Keep a few things in mind when looking for reviews:

- Don't expect your book review to appear in the major newspapers. Reviewers are sent hundreds of books each month and will choose the ones that appeal to them, usually books written by well-known authors or celebrities. Look for smaller publications and online sites.

- Don't expect all your reviews to be positive. Someone out there is going to dislike your book, and they will tell you so in their review. Don't forget you are asking for honest opinions.

- Don't put out a book that isn't ready to be published. This is vital! Make sure your book is professionally edited and filled with well-researched, accurate facts; a reviewer will cane you for too many typos, sloppy prose or inaccurate facts.

Here are some useful sites that can be used for book reviews:

Good Reads

This free site offers space where you can display your book and seek reviews. Join up with their Author Program and get your book in front of your target readers. They also offer the option to create an author bio page (see resources page).

Amazon

Whether you have your book for sale via the online POD/ ebook distribution channels or have your own Amazon account, readers can post reviews for your book on your Amazon book page. Once again, I must mention that all reviews may not be positive. So, if someone just didn't like your book, they can vent their feelings by posting a negative review on Amazon. Their comments will remain for all the world to see and cannot be removed (see resources page).

Google Books

Google is attempting to digitize and catalogue every book and make them freely available online. If your book will be available via the online POD/ebook channels, it will be listed automatically with Google Books (see resources page).

Social media networks

Social media networks such as Facebook, Twitter, Linkedin, YouTube, and Google+ are all free marketing platforms that are perfect for today's authors (see resources page for links to the following sites).

Facebook

Create an author page on Facebook, separate from your personal page (if you have one) and drive traffic to your book website. Search for groups you feel may be interested in your book and join them. A word of caution though, don't join a group and then go in with the big sell. You will alienate group members and likely get kicked out. Take a normal, casual approach by first introducing yourself, then getting involved with the group discussions, and gradually telling them about your book.

Seek 'likes' from wherever you can and regularly search for new like-minded friends. Use your page as you do your blog. In fact, your Facebook author page can be linked to your blog, so you need only post to one place. You can showcase events, such as book signings, and add photographs, as well as advertise upcoming events to all your friends and groups in one go. This is also a great way to advertise your book, but when taking advantage of this large, instant-access venue, always offer a buyer enticement, like a free chapter or ebook.

Instagram

Instagram is a photo and video-sharing social networking service owned by Facebook. This app allows users to instantly post images and information and can be a great platform for building a following and keeping your fans aware of your movements.

Twitter

Reach out to millions in 141 characters or less! Search and follow as many like-minded Tweeters or potential readers as possible. Tweet and re-tweet regularly. Similarly to Facebook, you can instantly advertise your book, notify your followers of upcoming events, and display linked snippets of your articles.

Linkedin

This platform has long been associated with business networking, but it is also a great resource for authors, as it is full of writer and author groups and forums. Linkedin is a gathering place for professionals who are accustomed to marketing, networking, and pursuing a business. Editors, authors, literary agents, Indie and small publishers, reviewers – avid readers – can all be found on Linkedin. As an author/publisher, you are now a business, of sorts, and this is a free, reputable venue to get your message out to people worldwide.

YouTube

More and more people are using YouTube as a search engine. To take advantage of this, open a free account, and then consider making and posting your own videos. These don't have to be epic movies at all, they can be simple and to the point, like a short PowerPoint presentation about your book. If you have done any author readings or special appearances, make sure you film them. A friend and your smartphone can be all you need for making quickie video clips such as you signing a book, thanking a fan, showing a book display. Have fun with it! You can also commission a video trailer for your book inexpensively or try making one yourself.

Google+

Google+ is similar to Facebook and Linkedin, but is becoming popular with the entertainment industry and performers. You can take advantage of the available contact and networking options, adding your updates and links – it's well worth your efforts (see resources page).

More and more social media sites are springing up every day. Enjoy discovering and joining those you feel will work for you, but make sure you are involved with the ones I've mentioned.

PUBLICIOUS IS HERE
TO HELP YOU!

If you have concluded that the process of self-publishing is too much for you to handle, that's quite all right. Publicious is here to help you!

We are experienced in the many steps and processes we've been discussing and every day we assist authors just like you.

We can take care of the entire self-publishing process from start to finish or you can choose the individual services you require. We provide the following professional services:

- Editing and proofreading
- Typesetting
- Book layout design
- Book cover designs
- Illustrations
- ISBNs, Library Catalogue and database listings
- Printing
- Ebooks
- Global Print On Demand (POD) online distribution

- Instant download ebook distribution from major online stores (Amazon, Apple iTunes, etc)
- Website design
- Book trailer videos

We would love to work with you and make your book/ebook the best that it can be.

On the following pages I have outlined our procedures and guidelines, which have been designed to assist you, our valued client, during our time working together.

1. Your Publicious Quote

All quotes supplied by Publicious are prepared individually on request. Quotes can be obtained by visiting the Publicious website http://www.publicious.com.au and filling in the quote request form or sending an email request to mail@publicious.com.au or telephoning Publicious on 1300 301 591.

All quotes are supplied with an agreement form and a current copy of the *Publicious Terms and Conditions*. All prices are listed clearly and individually, so you will know exactly how much cost is involved before you commit.

If, after the first contact, more information about the book is required, we will contact you by email to clarify our needs. We do this to ensure that we give you the most accurate quote possible. Quotes will usually be sent within 48 hours of the necessary information being obtained.

Please note: we calculate approximate page counts using 11.5pt Adobe Garamond Pro font and the size of the book required by the author. Page counts may vary at a later date if the author requires font size or margin changes. Font sizes and types for children's picture books need to be specified prior to quoting.

To accept the quote, the agreement must be signed and returned to Publicious along with the 1st instalment payment (see quote) transferred into the Publicious bank account or via Paypal before work will commence.

2. Publicious Editing Submission Guidelines

Editing, either by a Publicious editor or your own editor, must be undertaken prior to submission for typesetting or book layout.

If your manuscript will be edited by Publicious, the following guidelines apply for your document:

- A4 (US letter) Word document

- Double spaced, single-sided

- 3 cm (1.18 inch) margins all round

- Times New Roman regular 12 pt font

- All pages numbered

- Title and/or author's name on each page

Please contact Publicious if you need assistance with preparing your manuscript for editing submittal.

3. Publicious Typesetting and Design Submission Guidelines

(don't let any of the following procedures overwhelm you, we are here to assist and are only a phone call or email away.

Manuscript: submitted by email attachment, FTP upload, or memory stick.

Very Important! Once a manuscript is sent to Publicious for typesetting, the client acknowledges that the manuscript is a completed work (edited and proofread). Correction of errors, such as spelling and punctuation, are not a part of the typesetting process and must be completed before the manuscript is submitted. It is important to understand that any changes, other than formatting problems, requested after the typesetting has taken place will incur costs calculated at the current hourly rate, with a minimum charge of 1 hour.

Manuscripts ready for the final book layout (typesetting) should be submitted as a single-spaced A4 document.

Images: 300dpi resolution (or higher) jpegs submitted as zipped email attachments, FTP upload, disk, or memory stick.

Please do not paste photographs into the body of your text, as this will cause resolution loss during transfer.

To upload pictures to Publicious by FTP, go to this webpage and follow the prompts: http://www.publicious.com.au/Uploads.html

The password is: publicious.

Or you can use your own file transfer account.

Images should be numbered or named (e.g.: image1.jpg). Manuscripts with illustrations and/or photographs (images) should have the areas where images are to be placed clearly marked (highlighted if possible). Included should also be the image number/name, text/caption (if any) referring to the picture, and the image position:

Please contact us if you have any difficulties preparing or sending your images.

image1.jpg – caption (This is a picture of me) – centred

4. Getting started

Step 1 – *Book Information Sheet*

All Publicious books/ebooks are unique in one way or another and that's exactly how we like it! We don't use pre-made templates as a quick, cheap, and easy way to produce books; all our designs are created individually and with the author's input every step of the way.

Our *Book Information Sheet* is designed to ensure that our authors have the chance to tell us exactly what they want for their book. In the form of a Word.doc, the Sheet will be sent to you as an email attachment, inviting as much or as little input as you would like to offer. We would like for you to tell us of your vision for your book and its cover, so we can endeavour to reproduce your ideas as closely as possible.

Please note: if you are struggling for ideas for your cover design, that's quite all right, we'll work together to create the perfect cover for your book.

The *Book Information Sheet* also supplies Publicious with all the information required for the creation of your book, including: ISBNs (leave these areas blank if you don't have your ISBNs yet), print and distribution submissions, and any database entries.

If Publicious is supplying your ISBNs, we will need the following information via your *Book Information Sheet* as soon as possible for your ISBN application:

- Publisher name: (you are the publisher, but will you be publishing under a company name or your own name?)

- Author name:

- Book Title:

- Sub Title (if any):

- Address:

- Phone number:

- email:

- Web address:

- RRPs (Recommended Retail Prices)

  - Australia (AUD):

  - USA (USD):

  - Canada (CAN):

  - UK (GBP):

  - Europe (EURO):

- BISAC Headings – Your book will require a BISAC heading (category code) for your ISBN and any library databases or distribution listings you may choose to use. Choose up to 3 codes from the list that you feel are most representative of your book and include them in your *Book Information Sheet.* For a list of BISAC headings, visit: http://www.bisg. org/what-we-do-0-136-bisac-subject-headings-list-major-subjects.php

If you're not certain of what to list your RRPs at, look for books similar to yours in your local or online bookstores and price your book accordingly. Be realistic with your pricing, taking into account the economies and trends of the overseas markets when pricing in different currencies. Ebook prices should also be set at less than the print version of your book. Please remember: as the publisher, you are responsible for pricing your book.

Step 2 – Work commencement

On receipt of the signed agreement and the 1st instalment transfer, Publicious will issue a written receipt for any monies received as a PDF by email attachment. You will then be invited to submit your manuscript, your *Book Information Sheet,* and any images or illustrations to be used in your book. Please refer to the Publicious Submission Guidelines above for information on submitting manuscripts and images.

Publicious projects are issued on a first-come-first-serve basis, so after receiving your manuscript, images, and *Book Information Sheet,* your book will be placed in a queue. From that point, Publicious will endeavour to begin work on your book as quickly as possible.

Step 3 – Typesetting (book/ebook layout)

Once we begin the required work, we will design the first chapter of the book interior, including suggestions for title headers, fonts, and margins. On completion, a PDF 'proof' is sent to you as an email attachment for input and approval.

Your book has now arrived at what is called the first draft stage. This is where we invite your valuable input. You will be asked to check the headers, fonts, and margins. If there is anything you want to change, this is the time to do so.

After any necessary changes have been made, and you have approved the first chapter draft, Publicious will create a unique template from that draft and format the rest of the interior using that design.

Please note: changes to font sizes and spacing may increase the estimated page count, which could alter the final print and layout costs. We will advise you if such changes can or could affect your costs.

On the PDF proofs, you'll notice that there is no page number or header on the first page of the chapter (fiction only). This is traditional for novels and certain types of books and will continue like this throughout the book; however, it is not compulsory. If you prefer page numbers and headers at the beginning of each chapter, just let us know. This isn't usually the case with non-fiction.

On completion of the book's interior, a first draft PDF proof will be sent to you as an email attachment. At this time, you are invited to check the proof thoroughly and note any final changes that may be required to the layout.

Please note: all editing and changes to the text must be made prior to submission (see submission guidelines).

Step 4 – ISBN

An International Serial Book Number (ISBN) is required for all books and ebooks that are to be made available to the public for sale. A separate ISBN is also required for each individual format of the same book such as softcover, hardcover, ebook, and audio.

Please note: if you have a book and an ebook, we recommend purchasing a block of ten ISBNs. This works out to be the same price as two separate ISBNs and the remaining eight can be used for future books or editions.

If you already have your ISBNs, please include them on your *Book Information Sheet.*

If Publicious is supplying your ISBN or block of ISBNs, we will open an account with Thorpe and Bowker (ISBN Agency) in your name from the details supplied on your *Book Information Sheet,* and purchase your ISBN/block on your behalf once work on your book commences. You will immediately receive your ISBN/block by email and your log-in details, along with a receipt for payment. Please note: this is not an invoice; Publicious will have taken care of all payments regarding the purchase of your ISBN.

Once your book/ebook is complete, we will then use your log-in details to enter your Thorpe and Bowker account and allocate an ISBN to each book format.

To enable us to open your Thorpe and Bowker account, we will need the information listed under Step 1 via your *Book Information Sheet* as soon as possible.

Step 5 – Book Cover Design

Publicious will create the book cover design (where applicable) by blending images from our substantial image library (around 13 million images and photographs) or illustrations supplied by you or using original illustrations supplied by Publicious. (please see the illustrations page on our website for samples and pricing)

From the ideas you supplied in your *Book Information Sheet,* Publicious will produce a sample cover comprising a front cover, back cover, and spine calculated to the right thickness in relation to the page count and type of paper used for the interior. Samples will be sent to you as email PDF attachments for you to review and choose your preference.

Step 6 – Final Check

When your chosen cover has been completed, a final proof, along with the final interior file, will be sent to you for one final format check before printing.

Step 7 – Print ready proofs

On acceptance of the final proofs, Publicious will convert the files to high-res print-quality PDFs, submit them to the printers and place an order for your required quantity of books.

Step 8 – Printing

Please allow 2 - 3 weeks for delivery of printed books. If an advance printed proof copy is required, you should expect to receive the proof approximately 1 - 2 weeks after ordering. Then, there will be a further 2 - 3 weeks for the delivery of the ordered print run, from the time of proof acceptance. All deliveries will require a signature.

Please note: print turn-around times are estimates only and may vary.

5. Ebook Conversion

Step 1 – Unless you are providing Publicious with a PDF conversion-ready file, please see Steps 1 – 7 of the previous section (#4) for information on submitting your manuscript for typesetting. If you are supplying your own PDF, please skip on to Step 3 of this section.

Step 2 – A PDF of the book interior including the front cover will be created, then converted by Publicious to the ePub (iPad, Androids, Smartphones, Kobo, Nook, etc) and MOBI (Kindle) formats.

Step 3 – For authors supplying their own PDFs for ebook conversion, a single PDF will be required containing the front cover as the first page. There should be no blank pages and the imprint page should show the ebook ISBN - not the print ISBN. Please notify Publicious if you need an application for an ebook ISBN.

Step 4 – Once conversion is complete, a zip file containing a high-quality ePub and a high-quality MOBI file will be sent to you as an email attachment for your approval.

6. Print Only (For clients submitting pre-formatted print-ready files)

Step 1 – On acceptance of the Publicious print quote supplied to you, the agreement must be signed and returned and the full balance transferred into the

Publicious bank account before work can commence (bank details are listed just below the Publicious logo on your quote).

Step 2 – Submit your files for printing. Two high resolution PDFs, one for the cover and one for the interior, should be submitted to Publicious either as an email attachment, ftp upload, disk, or memory stick.

Interior PDF must be complete, the correct size for the required book including 3mm bleeds (if colour), include the correct book layout, the ISBN, and any extra information required, such as acknowledgements, dedications, etc. All fonts must be embedded and all images must be high-resolution (300 dpi or higher) CMYK.

Cover PDF must be minimum 300dpi resolution in CMYK and include the front, spine, and back cover. A 3mm bleed should be present with trim marks (unless otherwise specified) and your barcode should be in place.

Please note: the spine thickness must be calculated to match the overall total number of pages. If you are unsure of your spine thickness, please contact Publicious before submission and we will assist you in determining the correct thickness for your book's spine.

Step 3 – Publicious will submit the high-res PDFs to the printers and place an order for the required quantity of books.

Step 4 – Please allow 2 – 3 weeks for delivery of printed books. If an advance printed proof copy is required, you should expect to receive the proof approximately 1 – 2 weeks after ordering. Then, there will be a further 2 – 3 weeks for the delivery of the ordered run, from the time of proof acceptance. All deliveries will require a signature.

Please note: print turn around times are estimates only and may vary.

7. Print On Demand (POD) Distribution

With this distribution model, not only will your book be for sale on most of the major online bookstores, such as Amazon, Barnes and Noble, and The Book Depository etc, but it will also be available on the amazing 'Espresso Book Machine' at no extra cost (see link on Publicious website for further information).

Step 1 – Publicious will create high-resolution PDF/X cover and interior files to match the distributors' (Ingram Content Group) requirements and submit them, along with metadata, such as the international RRPs, discount rates (store mark-ups) and the book description (supplied by the author).

Please note: After submission, your listing will begin to appear on the online stores during the next 2 - 3 weeks. Once the listing is active, titles are ready to order.

POD distribution royalties and costs

The following is the breakdown formula used to calculate your book royalty:
- RRP (you set this price)
- Minus tax (10% GST for Australian sales only)
- = list price
- Minus discount 40% (recommended bookstore mark-up)
- = Wholesale price (list price minus discount)
- Minus print cost (deducted from w/sale value above)
- = Net royalty for self-published author (you)

Please note: Discounts (store mark-ups) can be set as low as 25% or as high as 55%; however, the lower figure may affect the title's desirability for listing by some book stores, where as the higher figure may attract more book stores. Please notify us which discount level you would prefer. Our standard discount (and recommended) setting for POD is 40%.

Each month a detailed sales statement will arrive as a PDF email attachment listing the amount of books you have sold in the previous month from the various markets.

Royalty payments are converted to your national currency (in line with current exchange rates at time of payment) and transferred directly into your bank account ninety (90) days after the end of the month that the sales were achieved (your bank details will be requested on the *Book Information Sheet*).

Please note: an annual listing fee plus tax will apply (see the Publicious terms and conditions), which will be due for renewal 60 days prior to the first anniversary of your book's submission into the POD distribution channels.

8. Ebook Distribution

This system works similar to the POD distribution model, but instead of your book being printed one at a time (at the time of purchase), they are made available for instant download from most of the online ebook stores including Amazon (Kindle). B&N (Nook), KOBO, Apple iTunes/iBooks, and Booktopia, etc.

The following is the breakdown formula used to calculate your ebook royalty:
  • RRP (you set this)
  • Minus discount 55% (fixed ebook stores' mark-up)
  • = Net royalty for self-published author (you)

Please note: Discounts (store mark-ups) for ebooks are fixed at 55% to ensure the highest possible exposure.

Royalties and monthly statements are issued in the same way as POD distribution.

Please note: an annual listing fee plus tax will apply (see the Publicious terms and conditions), which will be due for renewal 60 days prior to the first anniversary of your book's submission into the distribution channels.

Conclusion

We would love to work with you and help make your book the absolute best it can be. Remembering at all times that you are the publisher, not Publicious, this means you'll also have full control, retain all of your rights, and, by cutting out the middle man, you'll earn 100% of your royalties. However with the title of self-published author comes all the responsibilities of a publisher, including the marketing and selling of your book. This may seem like an overwhelming undertaking at first – but don't worry – we're here to help you every step of the way!

Good Luck!

Andy McDermott (Publicious Director)

PUBLICIOUS
BOOK PUBLISHING SERVICES

http://www.publicious.com.au

Like us on Facebook: http://on.fb.me/1bU3r4l
Folow us on Twitter: http://bit.ly/1jHhn1E
Join us on Linkedin: http://linkd.in/1i0YHN8
Google+: http://bit.ly/Nf5MeZ

Resources

PayPal

Australia: https://www.paypal.com/au

New Zealand: https://www.paypal.com/nz

USA: https://www.paypal.com

UK: https://www.paypal.com/uk

ISBN agencies:

Thorpe and Bowker (Australia) http://www.thorpe.com.au/en-AU/

National Library of New Zealand: http://natlib.govt.nz/forms/isn

Bowker USA: http://www.isbn.org/

Nielsen UK: http://www.isbn.nielsenbook.co.uk/controller.php?page=121

Prepublication Data Service (formerly CIP)

National Library of Australia: http://www.nla.gov.au/cip

National Library of New Zealand: http://natlib.govt.nz/forms/cip

US Library of Congress: http://www.loc.gov/publish/cip/

British Library: http://www.bl.uk/bibliographic/cip.html

Legal Deposit

Australia: https://www.nla.gov.au/legal-deposit

New Zealand: http://natlib.govt.nz/publishers-and-authors/legal-deposit

USA: http://www.copyright.gov/help/faq/mandatory_deposit.html

UK: http://www.bl.uk/aboutus/legaldeposit/

Book databases:

BowkerLink Book Database Worldwide:http://www.bowkerlink.com/corrections/common/home.asp

Nielsen Book Database:
Australia: http://www.nielsenbookdata.
com.au/controller.php?page=89

New Zealand: http://www.nielsenbookdata.
co.nz/controller.php?page=137

USA: http://www.nielsenbookdataonline.com/bdol/

UK: http://www.nielsenbook.co.uk/

Book Marketing:

The Book Marketing Network: http://
thebookmarketingnetwork.com/

89 Book Marketing Ideas that will change your
life: http://www.authormedia.com/89-book-
marketing-ideas-that-will-change-your-life/

The Authors Marketing Powerhouse: http://www.
theauthorsmarketingpowerhouse.com/

Book Marketing 101 | Jane Friedman : http://
janefriedman.com/2013/11/12/book-marketing-101/

Book Marketing Works: http://www.
bookmarketingworks.com/

Author Marketing Clubs: http://authormarketingclub.com/

Author Marketing Experts Inc. http://www.amarketingexpert.com/

WIX.com (free websites): http://wixstats.com/?a=3495&c=124&s1=

Google Adwords: http://www.google.com.au/

Social media links:

Facebook: https://www.facebook.com/home.php

Twitter: https://twitter.com/

Linkedin http://www.linkedin.com/

YouTube: http://www.youtube.com/

Google+ https://plus.google.com/

Instagram: https://www.instagram.com/

NOTES

_____

_____

_____

_____

_____

_____

_____

_____

_____

_____

_____

_____

_____

_____

NOTES

_____

_____

_____

_____

_____

_____

_____

_____

_____

_____

_____

_____

_____